Shaker Home

RAYMOND BIAL

Houghton Mifflin Company
Boston 1994

Library of Congress Cataloging-in-Publication Data

Bial, Raymond.
    Shaker home / Raymond Bial.
        p.   cm.
Includes bibliographical references.
ISBN 0-395-64047-4
        1. Shakers—United States—Juvenile literature.   [1. Shakers.]
I. Title.
BX9784.B53   1994   93-17917
289′.8—dc20   CIP
                            AC

Printed in the United States of America

HOR   10   9   8   7   6   5   4   3   2   1

Shaker Home is lovingly dedicated to my wife, Linda, and to my children, Anna, Sarah, and Luke, who accompanied me in taking the photographs in this book.

Whether wandering through the Shaker buildings, walking through a nearby woods brightened with wildflowers, or strolling around the grounds at dusk, being with them on these trips has been one of the most delightful experiences of my life.

Whether in Sabbathday Lake, Maine, or Pleasant Hill, Kentucky, Shaker villages seem far removed from the rest of the world. To the Shakers who once inhabited these places—and to the handful who still live in New England—each community served as a retreat from the world and the center of their universe.

Seen from a distance, a cluster of trim buildings is the first indication that the Shakers pursued a unique way of life. Not only are the buildings solidly constructed with thick stone foundations, but everything from the lines of the roof to the placement of the windows expresses simplicity and grace. The Shakers sought perfection in their lives, intending to create heaven on earth, and the buildings indeed have a light, airy feel about them. As one brother explained, "We think that man cannot hope to attain a spiritual heaven until he first creates a heaven here on earth."

Whether strolling along paths lined with trees, wading through the undulating green fields, or wandering through the buildings, a visitor can still feel the presence of the community of souls who once worked and worshipped in these villages. The efforts of the Shakers to create a perfect world—a utopian society—are reflected in everything from the elegant sweep of a picket fence to the ingenious workings of a door handle.

Known formally as the United Society of Believers in Christ's Second Appearing, the Shakers are the oldest communal society in America. For more than two hundred years they lived in these secluded villages, sharing quiet lives and striving for perfection

6

in every detail of living, from tending gardens to making furniture.

From Maine to Kentucky, Shaker communities once dotted the eastern half of the United States. Yet while the number of Shakers has declined, other people have become increasingly fascinated with their way of life. The Shakers have come to be widely admired, not only for their hundreds of clever inventions and their remarkable creations, but for their progressive values and beliefs. As Sister Frances Carr of Sabbathday Lake observes, "We'll go away in time, as will everybody. But our ideas and our way of life will never go away."

The Shakers were not always viewed so favorably. During the early years of their religion in the milltown of Manchester, England, they were persecuted. Even their name was originally a term of derision: some of the Shakers became so excited during their worship services that they would shout, tremble, and whirl about, "shaking" off their sins. Many of the early believers came from the Society of Friends, or Quakers, so they became known as the Shaking Quakers, later shortened to Shakers. Although the term was used in derision, the Shakers eventually adopted it themselves. They also refer to themselves as Believers or members of the United Society.

In 1758 the Shakers attracted a young woman named Ann Lees (later shortened to Lee). Married in 1762 to a blacksmith, she bore four children, three of whom died in infancy and the fourth as a small child. Always a spiritual woman, she turned to religion after these tragedies. In giving herself fully over to her faith, she declared, "My soul broke forth to God."

Ann Lee began to take an increasingly active role in the sect, notably speaking out against "cohabitation of the sexes." Meetings grew more animated, and opposition to them became so intense that at one point Ann Lee was imprisoned for "profanement of the Sabbath." Upon her release, she spoke of having had a vision of Christ. Given the name Mother, she became the leader and the spiritual force of the Shakers.

Because of their persecution in England, Mother Ann Lee and seven followers immigrated to the American colonies in 1774. They settled on land that is now known as Watervliet,

New York. For several years they scratched out a living, failing to attract new members. However, Mother Ann's charismatic personality gradually began to draw people. When Mother Ann died in 1784, at the age of forty eight, it was left primarily to James Whittaker, who had accompanied her from England, to build an organization that would sustain the fledgling society of roughly one hundred members.

Father James began the process of gathering the Shakers together in their own villages, apart from the "evils of the world." The year after Mother Ann's death, at the dedication of a meetinghouse in New Lebanon, New York, Father James introduced the "gospel orders." This formal set of rules for the Shakers included the complete separation of the sexes. Husbands, wives, and children were each placed in their own communal "families," with all property held in common. "All men shall come and go out at the west doors and gates; and all women at the east doors and gates."

Just three years after the death of Ann Lee, Father James himself passed away, leaving Joseph Meacham in charge of the village at New Lebanon, which had become the spiritual headquarters of the group. Father Joseph introduced a formal rule that all members "might have equal right and privilege, according to their calling and needs." He also selected a woman, Lucy Wright, to share leadership with him.

Joseph Meacham and Lucy Wright continued the separation of the Shakers from the world by organizing a number of independent villages scattered throughout New England. During

these years, so many people were joining the Shakers that large
communal buildings had to be constructed in the settlements.
By 1794, eleven villages had been established in New York,
Massachusetts, New Hampshire, Connecticut, and Maine. In

1805, when the Shakers heard of a revival sweeping the frontier, they sent out missionaries, and new communities were eventually formed in Ohio, Kentucky, and Indiana. At the height of the society's popularity, just before the Civil War, there was a total of twenty-four communities, with almost 6,000 members embracing the Shaker faith.

These Shaker villages were all similar, with buildings for particular uses: a place to sleep and to eat, a place to work, and a place to worship. The community itself was organized into "families" of fifty to one hundred brothers and sisters who shared a building with separate doors and stairways for men and women. Some of the stairs ascended in graceful swirls seemingly not of this world. Others were simpler, but in every case, men and women used separate sets of stairs. Each dwelling had its own sleeping quarters and dining room, where women and men sat apart, as well as its own kitchen, weekday meeting room, and perhaps an infirmary.

Anyone free of debt could become a Shaker. However, children and Shakers who had not yet made a full commitment to the faith formed a Novitiate Order. They often lived in separate buildings, apart from the rest of the village. However, those Shakers who had committed all their property to the society and fully accepted the Shaker way of life lived in the dwellings named according to their location in relation to the Center Family: West Family, East Family, and so forth.

Each family in the village was governed by two eldresses and two elders, who cared for the spiritual needs of the sisters and brothers. Deacons and deaconesses also helped to manage the

work assignments of each family. The eldresses and elders of the Center Family governed the village as a whole. Occasionally, several villages were joined under one ministry or bishopric. At the head of all the Shakers was the central ministry at New Lebanon.

Each family managed its workshops and tended its own crops, garden, and livestock. Occasionally, a family had its own schoolhouse and its own store for selling "goods," but generally the different families shared a common schoolhouse and other buildings, such as barns and shops. Most villages also had a trustees' house, where designated "trustees" sold goods to "the world's people," as non-Shakers were called. By allowing trustees to manage their business affairs, the other Shakers could remain separate.

The meetinghouse where the Shakers worshipped through song and dance on Sundays stood at the very center of the village. Shakers participated in services after breakfast and again following the noon meal. They spent the rest of the Sabbath refreshing themselves through meditation and relaxation. Like other Shaker buildings, the meetinghouse had separate doors for men and women. Although it was considered the most important building in the village, it was a plain structure and lacked the spire of traditional churches.

For many years, the Shakers not only recruited adult members but accepted orphans and children whose parents could not care for them. When they came of age, the children decided for themselves whether to leave the village or not. Other people joined the Shakers during hard economic times and bad weather. Appropriately called bread and butter Shakers or winter Shakers, they usually left when conditions improved outside the community. Many Shakers came and went over the years. Those who departed during the day were given provisions and a little money, but many others slipped off in the dark of night.

The Shakers may have been the most successful communal society in America, but given the size of the general population, their numbers, even in their heyday, were still quite small. Following the Civil War, the size of the sect steadily declined to only about a thousand members at the turn of the century. Now there are barely a handful. Over the years, the Shakers have been criticized for some of their beliefs, such as the separation of the sexes, the breaking up of natural families, and the communal sharing of goods. Difficulties also arose when a member

wished to leave the society and wanted property returned or compensation for work in the community. What was so appealing about the small Shaker sect that it is nonetheless held in such high esteem?

Today the Shakers are admired for their early belief in the equality of all people, regardless of race or sex. Their founder was a woman, and early in their history they were organized with both men and women as leaders. African Americans were welcomed into the society and a number of former slaves became members, especially in the South.

The Shakers were also committed to pacifism. They refused to take part in wars, from the American Revolution to the Civil War. During the Civil War, the Kentucky communities were frequently occupied and required to provide food and shelter for the armies of both sides.

Throughout the nineteenth century up to the present day, the Shakers have always been highly respected for their character, their way of life, and their humanity—all of which are clearly reflected in their surroundings and their many handiworks.

If they were going to separate themselves from the world, the Shakers knew from their early days at Watervliet that they would have to farm the land to make their villages self-sufficient. As one brother wrote in his journal, "Only the simple labors and manners of a farming people can hold a community together."

At first they barely survived, but gradually, through hard work, thrift, and the application of scientific methods, the Shakers brought their lands, in the words of one brother, from "rugged barrenness to smiling fertility and beauty." They sold their surplus farm produce to "the world's people." By the early 1800s, they also began to market goods put up in their kitchens, such as applesauce, dried apples, dried sweet corn, jams, and preserves.

At about the same time, the Shakers entered the garden seed business. They were among the first people to package seeds and earned a reputation for seeds of the highest quality. Within a few years they were peddling seeds on established routes from New England through the South. Also important was the growing of medicinal herbs. First published in 1831, their herb catalogue featured 154 different herbs, barks, roots, and seeds.

Just as they carefully tended their gardens and fields, the Shakers believed in raising the finest livestock. They were among the first people to breed farm animals scientifically, and they imported high-quality cattle and sheep from England to improve their herds. Further, they cared for their livestock as lovingly as they did everything else in their lives. As one brother wrote, "A man of kindness to his beast is kind. Brutal actions show a brutal mind."

The Shakers also became widely known for their inventive spirit. "A mania has seemed to take hold of some of the brothers for inventing and being skillful mechanics, and they are success-ful," a Shaker newsletter reported. "It is rumored that one of our members is now studying out a plan for a flying machine." Although it was left to the Wright brothers to perfect that inven-

tion, over the years the Shakers designed or improved hundreds of practical devices. They became so accomplished that people often assumed that any new invention was of Shaker origin. Just as the Shakers were generous to those in need, few of these inventions were patented so that they might be fully shared with the world.

Many of these inventions, such as the hay rake, mower, and a special plow for working on hills, helped the Shakers in their work. Among the many gadgets and tools in their workshops were the circular saw and an improved spinning wheel as well as a special loom for making narrow tapes for chair seats. Other inventions included the washing machine and several kinds of clothespins. The Shakers were also among the first people to use metal nibs in place of quills on their pens.

Much of the ingenuity of the Shakers reflected their deep sense of community and shared labor, as illustrated in their many inventions for the kitchen. Because the women prepared three meals a day for large groups of people, they devised many gadgets to lighten the work, including the slotted spoon, a pea-sheller, the cheese press, and a machine for washing potatoes.

When making large batches of pies, the sisters used double rolling pins to roll out twice as much dough. They also relied on an ingenious apple peeler with a screw handle and a corer. Sixty pies at a time could be baked in the large revolving ovens that they also invented.

The Shakers were committed to eating good, wholesome food; they believed that the soul could thrive only in a sound, healthy body. "It takes a whole man or woman to be a Shaker,"

they said, pointing to the longevity of their members. Frugal people, members were admonished to "Shaker your plates," which meant to clean them. The Shakers were among the first to use precise measurements of ingredients, and in 1796 they published one of the first cookbooks in America and became leaders in new techniques to preserve foods.

A notable tenet of the Shaker way of life was cleanliness. Mother Ann advised, "Clean your rooms well; for good spirits will not live where there is dirt. There is no dirt in heaven." The admonition was further reinforced by the Millennial Laws of 1821 (revised 1845): "No one should carelessly pass over small things, as a pin, a kernel of grain, etc. thinking it too small to pick up, for if we do, our Heavenly Father will consider us too small for him to bestow his blessing upon."

The flat broom, the most familiar Shaker invention, was put to such good use that it came to symbolize Shaker life. Daily cleaning actually began before breakfast, when the sisters swept their own and the brothers' rooms. Each day concluded with the brothers sweeping up their workshops.

The Shakers also installed wooden pegs on strips along each wall, usually about six feet from the floor. Chairs, brooms, hats, cloaks, and many other domestic articles were hung from the pegs to provide convenient storage and to make sweeping easier.

Chairs, tables, candle stands, and other furniture were designed to express the simplicity of Shaker life, as well as to ease dusting, and beds were fitted with rollers to facilitate cleaning under them. Often furniture, including chests of drawers and cabinets, were built directly into the walls so that they would not have any flat surfaces to collect dust.

The Shaker quest for perfection was also expressed in a sense of order. "A place for everything, and everything in its place," was a popular saying. Desks, chests, and tables had drawers for specific articles, whether needles and thread or packages of seeds.

Commitment for the Shakers began early in the morning—at four or five in the summer and an hour later in the winter. On rising, they knelt for a few moments in silent prayer, then the sisters tidied up the rooms and made beds. The sisters assigned to the kitchen started breakfast while the brothers did chores in the barns and planned the day's labor in the workshops.

At the ringing of the bell at six or seven o'clock, depending on the time of the year, the sisters and brothers gathered for meditation, then filed, women in one line and men in another, into the dining room. They took their separate places on either side of the room, offered a silent prayer, and quietly ate their breakfast.

Afterward, the children attended school or worked with the adults. (Girls attended school in the summer and boys, during the winter months.) The sisters set off for their assigned work in the kitchen, garden, dairy, laundry, or one of the workshops.

Although best known for their furniture and smallwares, the Shakers also practiced many traditional crafts, such as candle-making and spinning wool. The sisters might also package seeds or prepare herbal medicines.

Some of the men headed for the orchards, fields, or barns. Others entered the workshops, where they made chairs, tables, or perfectly symmetrical oval boxes. Or they might engage in traditional crafts, such as making brooms or buckets.

The Shakers switched jobs every couple of months so that they could enjoy some variety. Whatever the brother or sister was assigned to do, the work was satisfying and often related to the kind of work to which they were best suited. Seasonal work, such as gathering nuts and berries, husking corn, and making maple syrup also provided an enjoyable change of pace.

Not only were the Shakers surrounded by lovely objects of their own creation, but their rooms were filled with light and fresh air from large windows. Many doors had small window-panes that could be opened as well. "Fresh air is the Shaker medicine," a visitor observed.

The abundant light not only enhanced the quality of life, but allowed the Shakers to work without wasting candles and lamp fuel. What a contrast such rooms must have been to the dingy mills of Manchester. While the Industrial Revolution was sweeping across Europe and America and people were moving into a world of darkness in factories, subways, and mines, the Shakers worked quietly in brilliant light. Perhaps part of their appeal—then and now—is their ability to lead pleasant lives rooted in agriculture and cottage industries, creating good and useful objects with their own hands.

The Shakers valued every second of their lives. As Mother Ann Lee advised, "You must not waste one moment of time, for you have none to spare." At the ringing of the bell just before noon, the brothers and sisters paused for lunch; then they resumed their labors until they sat down to a light dinner around six o'clock.

In the evening a few tasks might be completed, after which the brothers and sisters withdrew to their rooms. News from other villages relayed in letters and through visitors was shared at these times. The brothers and sisters also worshipped or practiced dances. They usually retired for the night around nine in the winter and ten in the summer.

Occasionally, Shaker sisters and brothers met at union meetings. Sitting face to face at a distance of several feet, they discussed subjects of common interest or sang together, after which refreshments were shared.

Sunday services were devoted almost exclusively to singing and dancing. In their early years, the Shakers were known for whirling and free dancing, but by the 1820s their movements had become formal patterns, most often with brothers and sisters facing each other, hands cupped upward to accept gifts from God. Singing was very important to the Shakers, and several thousand gifts of songs were received by members through inspiration. Of these, "Simple Gifts" is the best known and perhaps most accurately captures the spirit of what it meant to be a Shaker:

'Tis the gift to be simple, 'tis the gift to be free,
'Tis the gift to come down where we ought to be.
And when we find ourselves in the place just right,
'Twill be in the valley of love and delight.
When true simplicity is gain'd,
To bow and to bend we shan't be ashamed,
To turn, turn will be our delight
Till by turning, turning, we come round right.

Although work and worship were blended into every detail of their lives, the Shakers also enjoyed many breaks from their daily routine, such as fishing, picnics, hiking, and carriage rides. They were also known to appreciate a little humor, even at their own expense.

In the early years, the Shakers had no clothing restrictions and simply wore the clothes they had brought with them. Later, dress codes specified color, material, and style, all Shakers dressing alike to emphasize the equality of the members of the community. Different garments were worn for work, every day, and Sunday. Although styles and colors varied over time, sisters generally wore long, plain dresses with pleated skirts, shoulder kerchief and cape, small white caps, and palm leaf or straw bonnets covered with silk.

Originally, like many colonial Americans, the brothers wore breeches and long hose, which were later replaced by trousers. Jacket colors varied over the years from gray to blue, with wide-brimmed hats made of wool, fur, or straw.

While the Shakers are interesting because of their unique way of life, they are perhaps best known for their many splendid creations, notably their furniture (including ladderback chairs, tables, candle stands, and desks) and smallwares (from baskets, barrels, and buckets, to nesting oval boxes). Mother Ann Lee urged her followers to "do all your work as though you had a thousand years to live on earth, and as you would if you knew you must die tomorrow" and "put your hands to work and your hearts to God."

Everything made by the Shakers was intended to be simple and practical. In their view, "Anything may be called perfect which perfectly answers the purpose for which it was designed." Yet the Shakers also expressed their devotion to God by striving for perfection in their handiworks. Edward Deming Andrews

described their work as "religion in wood," and Thomas Merton once said, "The peculiar grace of a Shaker chair is due to the fact that it was made by someone capable of believing that an angel might come and sit on it."

Today, Shaker furniture and smallwares are considered works of art and command very high prices at auctions. The few remaining Shakers are brokenhearted, because they did not create the objects to have material value. "I don't want to be remembered as a chair," lamented one elderly sister.

As a communal society, the Shakers shared all property, just as they lived together. What mattered to them was not the physical reality of the collection of buildings, furniture, and other objects, but the work and worship of their daily lives. As members of a communal society, the Shakers surrendered their individuality to the community. Choosing to be celibate, they gave up marriage and family, because in the mind of Mother Ann, they should live as brothers and sisters.

Many people think that the Shakers are dwindling in number simply because they did not marry and have children. Though children without parents were increasingly placed in orphanages, a larger cause was that by the late 1800s, Shaker communities could no longer compete in the marketplace with the low cost of goods mass-produced in factories. Also, following the Civil War, people were increasingly drawn to the bustle of growing cities, away from the quiet farms and villages that were the essence of Shaker life.

Mother Ann Lee predicted the decline of the Shakers: "There will come a time when there won't be enough Believers to bury their own dead. When only five are left, then there will be a revival." Perhaps the Shakers will again attract new members, but what is certain is that they have vastly enriched our world with the work of their hands and the beliefs of their hearts.

Further Reading

The following books were consulted in the preparation of *Shaker Home:*

Archambeault, James. *The Gift of Pleasant Hill: Shaker Community in Kentucky.* Pleasant Hill, Ky.: Pleasant Hill Press, 1991.

Beale, Galen, and Mary Rose Boswell. *The Earth Shall Blossom: Shaker Herbs and Gardening.* Woodstock, Vt.: Countryman Press, 1991.

Bolick, Nancy O'Keefe, and Sallie G. Randolph. *Shaker Inventions.* New York: Walker and Co., 1990.

Brewer, Priscilla J. *Shaker Communities, Shaker Lives.* Hanover, N.H.: University Press of New England, 1952.

Burns, Amy Stechler. *The Shakers; Hands to Work, Hearts to God.* Rochester, N.Y.: Aperture Books, 1987.

Butler, Linda. *Inner Light: The Shaker Legacy.* New York: Knopf, 1985.

Klamkin, Marian. *Hands to Work: Shaker Folk Art and Industries.* New York: Dodd, Mead, 1972.

Morse, Flo. *The Story of the Shakers.* Woodstock, Vt.: Countryman Press, 1986.

Neal, Julia. *The Shaker Image.* Boston: New York Graphic Society, 1974.

Sprigg, June. *By Shaker Hands.* New York: Knopf, 1975.

————. *Shaker Design.* New York: Whitney Museum of American Art, 1986.

Stein, Stephen J. *The Shaker Experience in America: A History of the United Society of Believers.* New Haven, Conn.: Yale University Press, 1992.

Van Kolken, Diana. *Introducing the Shakers: An Explanation and Directory.* Bowling Green, Ky.: Gabriel's Horn Publishing Co., 1985.

Acknowledgments

The photographs for *Shaker Home* were made at The Shaker Village of Pleasant Hill, Kentucky. I would like to express my deepest appreciation to the staff there for their generous help with this project and for their continuous efforts in keeping the spirit of the Shakers alive. Without the excellent work they do, day in and day out, none of the photographs in *Shaker Home* would have been possible.

I would also like to thank Audrey Bryant, Amy Bernstein, and the other staff at Houghton Mifflin for their efforts on behalf of *Shaker Home* and in support of my work in general.

As always, I offer my deepest thanks to my wife, Linda.